MW01170517

Poetic Outpouring Thoughts

(POTS)

BY

ESTHER RUTH BUTLER SIMS

Contact Information:
potserbs2023@gmail.com

Credits:
Cover Design: The Flying Idea
Graphic Illustrations: The Flying Idea
Photography: Validity Designs and Prints & Extended By Cae

ISBN: 9798853685581

CHAPTER
1

Adoration

Chapter Statements

Chapter 1:
ADORATION

God, our Creator, gets the glory for His marvelous creation.
We honor, admire, and praise Him for His magnificence and all His provisions.
We revere Him in the power of His work in using nature and individuals
to pronounce His awesomeness.

Chapter 2:
REFLECTING: MANIFESTATIONS, CHOICES, CHANGE, AND MOVING FORWARD

In reflecting upon God's existence, we accept the manifestations
presented and instilled within us to move forward, thus providing
more and greater productivity.

Chapter 3:
THINK ON THESE THINGS – REVELATIONS

As revelations are depicted, disarmament is in order...
and awareness blossoms

Chapter 4:
A SPOONFUL OF HUMOR

It is said that laughter is good for the soul; a merry heart is good medicine
(Proverbs 17:22). I agree, for laughter adds joy. Try it at some moment in
your life (perhaps today) as you allow laughter to sooth your soul.

Foreword

By Marshalita Sims Peterson, Ph.D.

Esther Ruth Butler Sims

Always writing – Always reading – With "book in hand" and Poetry "in thought".

Esther Ruth Butler Sims is indeed one who is passionate about poetry and she has gifted us by sharing her thoughts.

She is as a writer – a lover of words – a lover of recitation – a connoisseur of poetry. Mother's love of poetry has blossomed into her POTS – *Poetic Outpouring Thoughts*.

This book of poetry is crafted in expressiveness, admiration, honor, reverence, joy, celebration, love, passion, and yes, humor – the humorous spirit of Mother.

My sisters and I fondly remember and note to this very day Mother's love for Jesus Christ, Daddy, her three (3) daughters, sons-in-love, grandchildren, great grandchildren, AND her love of poetry. She had pinned hundreds of poems and plays through the years.

This is Mother and this book of poems is timely, thought-provoking, and relevant. The relevancy is quite interesting as she penned poems many, many years ago and as late as a few months ago – yet, the relevancy remains.

The presentation of this book of poems, *"Poetic Outpouring Thoughts"* is deliberately positioned in four (4) distinct areas and each represents "life thoughts" wherein you may actually relate in some way – simply, yet profoundly – you may see yourself. As you peruse and engulf yourself in POTS, note the triangulation and interconnectedness of Mother's poetic thoughts.

Chapter 1: Adoration
God, our Creator, gets the glory for His marvelous creation. We honor, admire, and praise Him for His magnificence and all His provisions. We revere Him in the power of His work in using nature and individuals to pronounce His awesomeness.

Chapter 2: Reflecting: Manifestations, Choices, Change, and Moving Forward
In reflecting upon God's existence, we accept the manifestations presented and instilled within us to move forward, thus providing more and greater productivity.

Chapter 3: Think On These Things – Revelations
As revelations are depicted, disarmament is in order... and awareness blossoms.

Chapter 4: A Spoonful Of Humor
It is said that laughter is good for the soul; a merry heart is good medicine (Proverbs 17:22). I agree, for laughter adds joy. Try it at some moment in your life (perhaps today) as you allow laughter to sooth your soul.

In closing, Mother has captured her gift of poetry writing which is quite a unique space; and at age 93, Esther Ruth Butler Sims continues to engage in POTS.

May the enduring and endearing legacy of Esther Ruth Butler Sims be delightfully impactful as she shares her passion – as she shares her literary gift – as she shares her POTS – *"Poetic Outpouring Thoughts"*.

CHAPTER 3
Think On These Things – Revelations

CHAPTER 4
A Spoonful Of Humor

Table Of Contents

CHAPTER 1
Adoration

CHAPTER 2
Reflecting: Manifestations, Choices, Change, And Moving Forward

DEDICATION

I dedicate this book of poems to my children, grandchildren and great-grandchildren.
I also dedicate this book to the memory of my late husband, Henry Marshall Sims,
the love of my life and the most wonderful husband ever –
God blessed me with Henry.
In addition, I dedicate this publication to my late parents, George W. Butler, II and
Esther L. Butler, the best parents one could find anywhere – such good, Christian
parental foundational training and love exhibited. Lastly, I dedicate this book of poems
to my siblings, extended family, friends and supporters throughout my life.

I honor God, my Savior and my Lord as it is because of Him that this book of poems,
"Poetic Outpouring Thoughts" is possible.

God, our Creator, gets the glory for His marvelous creation.
We honor, admire, and praise Him for His magnificence and
all His provisions. We revere Him in the power of His work in
using nature and individuals to pronounce His awesomeness.

In Adoration – Who Am I?

I'm the one who carried you – in my body you did thrive
Wondering and praying
When will you arrive?
 I am your Mother.

Believing in a Mother – Child bond
Even though a visual of me you did not see
Yet I talked to you – as you were a real part of me.
Your Mother – That's who I am.

I am the one – It's me
Who was filled with eagerness and with pain
Anticipatingly awaiting the sunshine and the rain.
Who am I? – I am your Mother.

Then God made it so – for all of us to know
Could hardly wait for your arrival
Praying faithfully for your survival.
Praise God – I am your Mother.

Continually prayed for you
I am the one who was so divinely blessed
Thankful to have you as my child – I eagerly confess.
A grateful Mother

To have you as my child – so very thankful am I
To see your darling, precious smile
Praise God – my dreams are realized.
A praying Mother

Prayer, praise, and anticipating your arrival
Oh how pleasant to hear your first baby cry
I kept repeating, "Thank You My Dear God"
With a prayerful sigh.
I am your Mother.

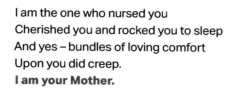

I am the one who nursed you
Cherished you and rocked you to sleep
And yes – bundles of loving comfort
Upon you did creep.
I am your Mother.

Loving you at all times and in all seasons
In the middle of the night, your diapers I did change
And the pillows on your bed I did rearrange.
For I am your Mother.

Time passes and I see you advancing
On your first day of school, you made me shed a tear
To see you, my baby leave me in the rear.
I am your Mother.

That simply meant for me
That you were growing up
You'd drink now from a glass and not from a baby cup.
Your Mother – I am.

I was right there for you
All through your school age years
Through love, discipline and support you did get my cheers.
Who am I? – Your dedicated, loving Mother

In adoration and awe, I poured out my love to you
You were a sweet, adoring child
Rather playful, conscientious, and mild.
Who am I? – An affectionate Mother

I watched and nurtured you
But when you broke the rules, something had to be done
And as your loving Mother, this game I always won.
A watchful Mother

Sometimes over in the night when you were not home – not in
I would pray to God in earnest
That His grace on you He'd send.
A praying Mother

Yes, God knows me as a worrying Mother
For your safety – I was constantly in prayer
In belief and faith – that your life He would spare.
Who am I? – A Mother who talks to God all of the time

I continually pray and trust – remembering my task given role
To help and support one another
And that of being a Christian Mother.
Who am I? – I am your Mother.

I find myself going to church and giving away my time
With multitasking as life goes
Involved with books, papers, and prose.
Who am I? – A busy Mother

To do as one should,
I try serving in different capacities
And as various needs appear
In service and dedication to others – encouragement and a bit of cheer.
Who am I? – A servant Mother

But of all my numerous activities, tasks, and requests
The essential and one thing I really crave
Is for Christ your soul to save.
Who am I? – I am Your Mother.

What A Mighty God We Serve

Gazing at His greatness as I sit among His breeze and taking breaths of holiness
While gazing at His glorious creation with trees swinging to and fro
And the blue skies interspersed with milky looking clouds – I hear an echo.
"What a mighty God we serve".

The tall pines, oaks, and different tree breeds
They provide homes and nests for creation unannounced
For God has established jobs for them
And God's beautiful splendor responds to His call,
I can hear a quiet whisper, "What a mighty God we serve."

God may not be physically talking, but we note His work in progress
We see and hear the brown rustling leaves all shattered on the ground
As we walk through the forest admiring His works.
And then suddenly something streaks across the sky,
That something has lights that fly quickly by leaving us in wonder,
"What's going to happen?"
Responding quietly, within my system, my response,
"What a Mighty God we serve."

When I say, "I see the lightening flash and I hear the thunder roll."
I behold God watering the parched grass for me in my front and back yards.
And with the cool water casting down upon my dried-up flowers and the drooping
Vegetables perking up after swallowing gulps of water from the rainy skies, my heart
Calls out in gratitude, "What a mighty God we serve."

The how, when, where, and what surfaced before I could finish questioning
This skylight wonder as my ears popped open to a thunderous sound.
Could it be a sign of what's about to come?
Of nature being evidence of God's workmanship?
Is God amazing or what?

I reflected on nature – its provisions and beauty and I stopped and praised God which
Was an overdue duty. For this world that I'm in – that I take so much for granted – a
World that is straight, bent, round or with a curve, my heart constantly reminds me,
"What a mighty God we serve."

Reminding myself – for out of the clay, He made me and equipped me with knowledge,
Feet and hands to use – all for His glory.
And in settling off to sleep, I ponder with a mind full of wonder.
I doze off in the great beyond with a clouded head, a quieted mouth,
But with a strong belief and a heartfelt trust that I will be better
Someday and look toward tomorrow.
All because of His greatness – "What a mighty God we serve."

Amazing Grace – Amazing He Is

"Amazing Grace" is what we sing
 For we are recipients of His care and love.
"Amazing Grace" is what we say
 His many blessings are sent from above.

God's kind mercy and his loving grace
We really do receive and believe.
His boundless graciousness
His sure support, we do conceive.

With God's good grace, love, and mercy
On Him we do depend.
For He has promised in His word
He'll be with us to the very end.

So, it's positively assuring
That His promises are true.
He's on duty 24-7
We're witnesses of what He'll do.

His A*mazing Grace* is evidence
And there is nothing like His love.
For we are showered with His blessings
Around us, under us, and above.

His A*mazing Grace* is so powerful
And He knows that we are humanly weak.
Despite our limitations
God's blessings we commonly seek.

It's *Amazing* how things work
For God has a direct plan.
As His followers and His children
Many things we don't understand.

Yes, it's *Amazing* and we're so blessed
God's omnipotence is clearly seen.
He uses His power every hour
For on Him we have to lean.

Amazing He is and we know it
And to Him we humbly bow.
Asking God to please help us
For He knows when, where, and how.

Amazingly He answers
In His own manner each day.
For He is divine, and His light does shine
And He responds in His God-given way.

You may look high, or you may look low
You may look anywhere on this sod.
But you won't find anyone compared to
Our *Amazing Loving God*.

Tips For God – Honoring Him

Tips – Tips – Tips
To support a service we endear
Tips for this and tips for that
We tip hardily with a smile and a cheer.

For all that good service
We received in the restaurant
Someone behind the guest scene
Provided money without a haunt.

Even though God has reminded me
That the tenth of my salary is His
I think of His many provisions
That bring me to tears.

I should willingly honor Him
And do it with obvious cheers
For the love He shows as the bright light glows
Yes, He has done this for many years.

For the numerous gifts from our great Provider
Our thankfulness should be more than our lips
For the life that we live and the love that He gives
We should honor Him beyond mere tips.

There should be no slips
That our pocketbooks will allow
When it comes to God's tips
Far more than just tips are due to our God right now.

Beholding Nature

Walking outside and beholding
Inhaling and exhaling a blessing
I don't need to stop and wonder
Nor send my mind out a guessing.

As I walk outside and think
And I see myself a sniffing
Fragrances of the outside world
And little animals just a riffing.

Without any voices singing
Without anybody muttering
I silently behold God's splendor
And I hear no uttering.

There is no writing or any scribbling
Nothing is pinned down
Just breathing in the air and thinking
Of this quiet little country town.

Oh how beautiful and so exquisite
Is this lovely world
How God in His image included nature
He formed, He created, He impearled.

Looking at this magnificent world
And this green grass on which I trod
It's the product of our Creator
And the work of our great God.

Above my head are many trees
With leaves swinging to and fro
I see bushes on my level
Some close up and others near my toe.

And standing still looking up high
I see white clouds in the sky
They are slowly moving as they pry
For God's creation is moving by.

When you go outside and ponder
And just look gracefully around
You may see trees swaying
Coming up from the ground.

Some may have birds
Some may be just plain bare
But they are God's creation
Planted especially for there.

Sometimes I think of the beautiful seasons
With each holding its own
And of God's handiwork of nature
And of the seeds He has sown.

There are four seasons in the year
And each has a purpose for me and you
God planned it with precise intention
And He gave each one its special clue.

The early season is spring
It arises from its winter sleep
It rested its livelihood
So good products they would reap.

Beautiful flowers in different varieties
Are caught in breathless awe
People talk to them and walk with them
And share what they see or saw.

Then summer comes and is awaiting
With its summer warm beams in place
Summer avails much on special terms
And provides beauty edged with lace.

Nature is absolutely gorgeous
It holds off summer until the fall
Then down it'll come patiently from
Obeying God's heavenly call.

Fall's attention to timely colors
Often begins a brand-new season
Yellow, orange, black, and brown
Personified colors reveal the reason.

And now introducing resting time
And getting prepared for the cold
Maybe holidays involved
Each playing a major role.

Oh, such beauty everywhere
Some natural and lofty creations
God-given talent expressed
As we behold the innovations.

The lighter holly bushes
And cedars taken from their nests
All beautiful and glorified
In their ornaments all dressed.

Nature did its part with wisdom
The resources it provided
Then man moved forward diligently
On what nature had decided.

Pine straw, pine trees and the like
Were used inside and out
Those talented decorators
All deserve a sincere shout.

Winter closed out the season
Though nature has no rest
It humbly and quietly supplies
Resources so we'll be blessed.

"Come Eat P's With Us"

"Come and eat some **P**'s With us, they'll make you big and strong.
When you really eat and digest them, I **P**romise you won't go wrong."

The first thing on our table, is a **P**raying **P**rayer **P**artner.
For **P**rayer will give the blessing as we ask God to meet us here.

Practical **P**eace is being **P**rovided, it's a needed special dish.
Tasty **P**ositivity is available and **P**reparation we dare not miss.

Pleasantness is the appetizer and **P**atience **P**rojects the way.
Now **P**rudence and **P**erseverance are **P**arts of the main entre'.

We wait **p**atiently for **P**atience for **P**roper **P**reparation has been made.
Progress has our stomach awaiting and **P**rosperity on the **P**latter is laid.

Personality is the appealing topping which gives that extra taste.
And it **P**rovides the special **P**ower that thoroughly cooks down the "**P**" base.

Humble **P**rogress steamed from **P**runing and in the **P**assion bowl.
Is the aromatic smelling organized **P**lanning that made this "**P**" dinner whole.

Because these "**P**s" were **P**repped and on the "**P**" table for this hour.
You are encouraged to eat and enjoy this food and be a witness of this "**P**" **P**ower.

This "**P**" menu is from my heart; it's intangible, but it means a lot.
Forgetting the **P**ower of words and actions – I certainly cannot.

Yes, these "**P**"s if ingested are correctly digested when you chew.
Undoubtedly, time will tell what "**P**s" can do for you.

Back To The Basics

Grace – Peace – Mercy – Gratitude – Prayer

The foundation and **basics** of God
Should hold a special place.
For in our heart and soul
He resides and is our solid base.

In analyzing the **basics** of God
We can think of a base, a starting point and foundation.
And all are applicable
For our spiritual elevation.

Yes, it means our Christ-like foundation
On which our faith is built.
That firm, sturdy, and fundamental base
This foundation will certainly not fall or tilt.

The **basics** of the Bible
Include God's grace and peace.
So cast your cares upon Him
For His mercy will never cease.

Christ – our foremost leader and Saviour
So in life – no need to stumble and hide.
Our **basic**, sure, foundation is constant
Our Heavenly Father – our guide.

In spite of challenges and questions
And in spite of actions we seek to defend.
Let's keep it **basic** and simple
It is on Christ we can depend.

In closing this **basics** refrain
Give thanks with a grateful heart.
This should be our utterance
Prayer and gratitude each day from the start.

Gratitude Is On My Plate And I Thank You

Gratitude is on my plate and
I can hardly wait
To share my gratitude
For your lovely attitude.
And I thank you.

A heart of gold and sincerity
Through and through
And like sisters and brothers
You're always helping others
And I sincerely thank you.

You didn't have to help me
And you did not have to listen
But you willingly shared
And graciously showed that you cared.
I thank you.

You could have kept your time
And not focus on interacting with me
But instead, you engaged
And embraced me tremendously
And I thank you.

You are helpful, kind and supportive
With a God-given art
May God bless your wonderful, serving heart
Please know that I thank you.

God Sees, God Knows

For the paths that I take
And the roads I chose
All remind me that
God sees and God knows.

Sometimes in situations
In our highs and in our lows
Confrontation may make or break us
But, God sees and God knows.

For if you have a problem
And the answer comes and goes
Talk to our Heavenly Counselor
For He sees and truly knows.

Let's be honest with ourselves,
Let's check our hearts and our souls
For everything that we do
God sees and God knows.

What Did He Leave Me?

For those many years I lived with him
And I can see him as plain as day.
And during this period of time
I recall much of what he'd say.

During that period of time
I never saw him standing up straight.
For his back was afflicted
That was a permanent physical fate.

In spite of this physical handicap
That doesn't linger much on my mind.
But how he taught, trained,
And disciplined us
Is an everlasting find.

He had very little money stored away
But that didn't seem to bother him.
For his focus was on character building
To Daddy, that was a precious gem.

Truly serving our Almighty God
In each and in every respect.
Our household under Daddy's control
Was his command and what he'd expect.

In disciplining by what he stood for
And how much faith he had.
He was concerned about how we lived
And all of that was left by Mother and Dad.

What did he leave me, I keep querying
The answer is clear and true.
It's the morals demonstrated
That anyone could plainly view.

Integrity and such wisdom
And a desire for holiness.
Respect for humanity
Laid heavily on his chest.

He left forgiveness and much kindness
And a desire for honest discretion.
And within our household he left for us
Biblical knowledge with an honest expression.

Not a physical inheritance
But from his Christian heart.
He left a spirit of Bible teaching and learning
From which I can never ever depart.

What did Daddy leave me?
That keeps popping up in my head.
This question was asked by an innocent child
It makes us reflect on my devotional daily bread.

Well, my loving father left for me
A wealth of sincere trust.
Self-respect and obedience
Faith and honesty, a sure true must.

Respect for God's Holy Word
And cleanliness with a life of hope.
Parental training to be followed
On issues for which to cope.

Summing up Daddy's attributes
That he wanted his children to embrace.
Were not the things that money could buy
But rather, a Christian foundation and base.

For in the Book of 1st Corinthians
And that which is found in Chapter 13.
This directory of LOVE is an inheritance
Our keepsakes on which to lean.

Daddy didn't have loads of money to leave for us
In fact, a simple yet, powerful man indeed.
His inheritance – he wanted his children all saved
For that was his prayer and creed.

So, I'm grateful for such an inheritance
Of the most important in his will
The most precious of it all
Is God and Daddy's desire of my salvation to fulfill.

How Much Do I Owe?

How much do I owe you?
That's rather easy to figure out.
It would take less than a minute
Certainly without a doubt.

How do I repay you?
And when shall I begin?
How much do I owe you?
For You have covered our burden of sin.

How much do I owe Him?
Is my constant mental and spiritual call.
My answer to this question
May seem so very small.

But when I truly respond
There simply is no real way.
For I owe everything to Him
The sum I certainly cannot pay.

How much do I owe You?
It's reverbing – resonating in my soul.
How much do I owe You – my Savior?
My gratefulness, I can't seem to control.

I owe Him everything
That's so plain to see.
For He is the Author
Of His magnificent creativity.

Regardless of how I may try
I cannot truly pay God and here's why.
For He is beyond measure and repayment
His love, grace, and mercy – is my earnest cry.

My repayment is to serve and obey Him
This is my task and charge.
For I owe Him everything
Remaining thankful – for my heart to enlarge.

How much do I owe You?
For in my very existence.
Indebted I am forever
And with all of my persistence.

I ask – How much do I owe You? … and How can I repay you?

Seeing God Through "C's"

CREATE within me a clean heart
CULTIVATE pure love from Thee.
CHASTISE me when sins creeps in
For I know all power is from Thee.

CONSECRATE my soul into righteousness
And sunny days from Your light.
COMFORT me from ailing pains
And let my work be bright.

COME into my heart, Lord Jesus
And make me truly whole.
CHANGE my heart and my mind
And please, save my soul.

CONSIDER my numerous paths
The sweet ones and the bitter.
Please **CHOOSE** the right
Passageway for me
And downcast those filled with litter.

CONDONE not evil planters
And the holes they dig for others.
For those diggers may fall
Into those same holes
Rather than their sisters and brothers.

COURAGE invites one to be strong
For there are decisions we face each day.
For the Bible tells us to be **COURAGEOUS**
As Jesus will pave the way.

CUT off our strings of sin
For sin likes to keep holding on.
Lord, may we ignore such temptations
And trust You – our Holy One.

CONSECRATE me, Lord, for Your service
And Satan will flee from me
I seek to honor Your Word and way
For that is my earnest decree.

By **CONCENTRATING** on Your word
And going to You in prayer.
All of that enables us
And assures us that You care.

When I **CONTEMPLATE** how Satan works
And how he tries to win me over.
I think of God's **CONSOLATION**
And I revere Him as my Maker and Molder.

COUNCIL us, Lord, we pray
We need Your direction and advice.
There are so many harmful distractions
That are destructive and not nice.

Sin can be so enticing
And it needs to be **CAST** away.
And buried with the filth
In the grave of deathly decay.

So **CREATE** within us, dear Lord
A **CLEAN** purified heart.
May we follow Your Word and teaching
And never from You depart.

CHANGE me into righteous living
And circulate Your blood in me.
For You died a Holy death
So we could all be free.

These "C's" are giving us **COMMANDS**
And we need to listen well.
The scripture is based on Psalms 41:10
In our hearts, this scripture should dwell.

So **CROWN** us LORD with your **CLEANLINESS**
With **CARING** minds of **CALVARY.**
COMMITTED spirits and the **CROSS**
Preparing us for a **CHRIST-LIKE** foundation
And for eternity.

CHAPTER 2

Reflecting: Manifestations, Choices, Change, And Moving Forward

In reflecting upon God's existence, we accept the manifestations presented and instilled within us to move forward, thus providing more and greater productivity.

March On Women, March On

March is National Women's Month
And, oh how proud we are
That women are given recognition
And have lifted the bar quite far.
March On Women, March On

In our nation and throughout the world
There is still some segregation
There is racism, culturalism and genderism
There is a lack of integration.
March On Women, March On

Focusing on women's progressions
They work hard, but are treated unfairly
Though their feelings have been aired and their work has been compared
They have been overlooked quite clearly.
March On Women, March On

It was in the 1980's under President Jimmy Carter
That during the month of March
We would establish a special torch
In recognition of women's super services whether old or a new starter.
March On Women, March On

Success and achievements stare many women in the face
They are given empowerment
And supporting endowment
And a most desiring embrace.
March On Women, March On

Now March is the right month
For women are marching on
March is the right month
As their leadership is being shown.
March On Women, March On

Today, women are marching right
They are marching day and night
There is proof in the pudding
That they are marching for what is right.
March On Women, March On

Let's honestly face it
Women are continually growing
And we all are reaping benefits
From the seeds they are sowing.
March On Women, March On

Speaking of the seeds
From which tall trees grow
Our hearts can reflect and also interject
How women have challenged untiringly the stressful upward flow.
March On Women, March On

You see, God knew what He was doing
He knew how, when, and where
When He took the rib from Adam
And made a female clear and fair.

He knew man needed help
For he needed so very much
A help meet, help mate and supporter
Man needed a female touch.

So he pondered over His son, Adam
And took a rib from Adam's side
And He shaped a female image
With these thoughts, He complied.

God put smart brains in the woman's head
He endowed her with fortitude
He embraced her with skills galore
For any challenging interlude.

He designed her to nurse her offspring
And give them maternal care
And that special infantile touch
That only a mother can share.
So Women Began Marching

Today's woman is different
From what she used to be
She is so much more involved
And displays expanded vitality.

Leadership roles are evident
In all phases of our lives
We are abundantly blessed and challenged
When each successful day arrives.
March On Women, March On

Truly, women should keep on marching
There are leadership roles in numerous spaces
Globally, nationally and on the local scene
There are female leaders in many places.

Women, we are grateful for your services
You deserve commendation
Whether we want to acknowledge it or not
Women are the backbone of our nation.
March On Women, March On

And speaking of our nation right now
We're reflecting on our Federal Court
We are thinking of a superbly prepared woman
It's Judge Jackson and she gets a wealth of support.
March On Women, March On

You see, it's organizations like NAUW
And like NCNW, too
And other supporting groups
Who share the women's progressive view.

For March is the right time
It is month #3
Full of notable facts
It is the month succeeding our Black History.
March On Women, March On

March is the right time
It follows the month of love
It calls our attention to
The genius of women from God above.
March On Women, March On

March is a unique and distinct time.
March is the bright time.
March is the height time.
March is the sight time.
Yes, March is the right time.

So, women, keep on marching.
Whether it's month 1, 2, or 3.
For the Father, Son, and Holy Ghost
Like us, they are supporting thee.
March On Women, March On

Walking In The Promises Of God

Have you ever been walking forlorn?
Have you ever been talking alone?
And wondering what to do?
Well, pause a bit
And then admit
God promised to see you through.

Have you ever been in trouble?
And life seemed like a struggle
And you are wondering what to do?
Well, seek God's peace
And ask for his release
God promised to see you through.

Life is surrounded by its twists and turns
It's a bitter sweet that also burns
And you start wondering what you must do
Then, get on your knees
Tell God about these
For God promised to see you through.

Walking in the promises of God
May seem to be long and hard
And you're still wondering what to do
Just be patient and wait
Until God opens the gate
For God promised to see you through.

By waiting and by walking
And not by any stalking
You'll find heartfelt peace
That will not cease or decrease
God's word is true, it's no tale
God's word is true, it cannot fail.
Just Walk in the Promises of God.

A Change Is Coming

Get up! Get out! We have arrived
All of your sleeping naps
Have now been denied
We're now in America, land of the free
Much uninhabited land
You will now see
Is this the new justice, you're talking about?
That you say is coming without any doubt.

Justice and change? Just what do you mean?
I've been around a long time and life ain't so clean
I've seen how, when, and where, I've been a victim all of my life
Filled with denial, misery and strife.
There will be justice. A change is coming.

That's easy to say; but hard to see
When I behold different blessings all around me
I'm like a forbidden person; I can't even express myself
My prayers are hung up high, way up on the shelf.
There will be justice. A change is coming.

I'm so different now with my head in the sand
I find myself struggling, and doing the best that I can
Different because of my pretty brown skin
Different because of the neighborhood I'm in
Or maybe because of the styles of my hair
And someone may be wishing and feel some jealousy there.
But there will be justice. A change is coming.

Living in my past should not be the rule
Or trying to persuade me that education is not cool
I was told by some that I didn't even need
To write, to think, or to plan, nor focus on how to read
They tried to make me believe that crazy phrase
But something within me said those are useless ways.
For there will be justice. A change is coming.

Justice, I keep thinking, just what does it really mean?
Just righteous, just fairness just life that is clean
Just an opportunity to do what is right
Just using the brain that God has endowed in my sight.

Justice is following the Bible for God's word is so true
Justice is doing unto others as you want them to do unto you
Justice is fair education with no degradation
No false separation but honest integration.
Justice is on its way. A change is coming.

A change is coming and we are part of it
No longer will we just talk and sing and sit
We have sat down too long and let our rights slip by
And now a new day has approached and God is showing us why
And today man is listening and to us God is speaking
And He is admonishing us that we should keep on seeking.
Justice is on its way. A change is coming.

Actually, changes have started coming our way
Strong men, strong women – strong voices are leading us today
They remind us of the rules found in our constitution
Showing us all, white, brown, and black of our overdue restitution
Even though our major parties are often politically split
We need to patiently seek how God's plan will surely fit.
Justice is on its way. A change is coming.

Just look at our White House; observe what God has done
Giving us more leadership roles elevating us one by one
A Black President elected in the year of 2008
His name is Barak Obama who was and still is superbly great!
Justice is on its way. A change is coming.

Our justice thoughts keep coming and justice will not sway
Therefore, we must be vigilant for a change is on its way
Blacks are continually rising, yes, justice is on its way
A change is constantly coming, we are testimonies of it today.
Justice is on its way. A change is coming.

Forward Moving – Forward Moving
A prepared Black woman is now in the Vice President's chair
She is Kamala Harris and she is precociously bright
Prudent, prepared, and progressive, for she will do what's right.
Justice is coming, a change is on its way.
God has everything planned for us just let Him have His say.
Justice is coming, this truth comes from the soul
Believe, beware, behold.
Watch our God who is in control. A change is coming.

A Tribute To
Dr. Martin Luther King, Jr.

Martin Luther King, Jr. was not born
With a silver spoon in his mouth.
He came from humble working parents
From the state of Georgia and that is in the South.

And here we are in 2023
Still striving to survive.
The inspiration that Dr. King gave us
Is helping to keep his dream alive.

How do we know his dream is still alive?
Well, since his passing in 1968
Significant black progress has been made
As we acknowledge efforts to this very date.

SONG: May The Work I've Done Speak For Me

Efforts and actions such as a Black United States President
Whose name is Barak Obama.
He is respected, honored and admired
Over the nation and its panaroma.

Changes galore with Dr. King's dream still alive
As we continue to bask in the sun.
For Kitanji Brown Jackson – an outstanding Black female
Our first Black Federal Supreme Court Justice – and she was indeed the one.

Martin Luther King, Jr. did not advocate
An eye for an eye or tooth for a tooth.
But he sought to turn violence into love
Which demonstrated peaceful truth.

He took abuse and more abuses
Yet justice to each person he'd bring.
A super civil rights leader
That was Dr. Martin Luther King.

Now when we think of Dr. King
Our minds think of justice and a change.
Yes, a change is coming
Whether short or long range.

SONG: Ain't Gonna Let Nobody Turn Me Around

Yes, a change is coming – Justice
There will be justice. A change is coming and we shall overcome.

Justice, I keep thinking, just what does it really mean?
Just righteous, just fairness, just life that is clean.

Just an opportunity to do what is right.
Just using the brain that God has endowed in my sight.

Justice is following the Bible for God's word is so true.
Justice is doing unto others as you want them to do unto you.

Justice is fair education with no degradation.
No false separation but honest integration.

Justice is on its way. A change is coming and we shall overcome.

A change is coming and we are part of it.
No longer will we just talk and sing and sit.

Actually changes have started coming our way.
Strong men and women – strong voices are leading us today.

They remind us of the rules found in our constitution.
Showing us all of our overdue restitution.

Justice is on its way. A change is coming and we shall overcome.

Blacks are continually rising; yes, justice is on its way.
A change is constantly coming; we are testimonies of it today.

A change and justice are coming; this truth is from the soul.
Believe, beware, behold and watch our God who is in control.

Our justice thoughts keep coming and justice will not sway.
Therefore, we must be vigilant for a change is on its way.

So today, we are listening as we know God is speaking.
And in honor of Dr. King and our progressive seeking.

We proclaim – **Justice is on its way. A change is coming and we shall overcome.**
SONG: We Shall Overcome – A Change Is Coming
         A Change Is Gonna Come – Oh Yes, It Is

Choose Your Words

Colossians 4:4-6 | *Psalms 139:1*

I can make or break friends
By the way that I walk
I can make or break friends
From the way that I talk.

My daily conversation
Should always be full of grace
It should be constantly filled with salt
To give the delightful taste.

Words, however, can be evil
And filled with ugly greed
Or maybe envy, murder or strife
That provided an ugly lead.

Harshness, negative tone and deceit
These qualities should not be hung
For maintaining good friendship
They should not be on your tongue.

Read Colossians 4:4-6
And Romans 1:29
Meditate, pray, and think of these
For a good friendship line.

The tongue can be a destroyer
And often brokenness it brings
Division and unhappiness
And misery sometimes it clings.

But Paul in the Bible advises us
In many of his letters
Of how to get along with others
And we'll become friend setters.

In the Book of James
It's in Chapter 3
He, too, gives advice about the tongue
So careful we should be.

In Psalms 139 David made a reference
Read it carefully and you'll see
"Before a word is on my tongue
Lord, know it completely."

When talking with others
We shouldn't talk too soon
Nor talk too much
But in a Christian tune.

The engrafted word should be heard
This Word of God is really true
It shall not be denied, but be our guide
For it was designed for me and you.

Lord, Please Revive Me

Lord Jesus, Now Lord, I come to you
For a very special visit
For I need the personal guidance
Of you precious Holy Spirit.
Lord, Please Revive Me.

I know I need anointing
You said so in your word
Zechariah 4:6 says
"By my spirit", saith the Lord.
Please Revive Me Dear Master.

Father, you know my heart
What more can I say?
Lord, take me, make me, use me.
And Revive Me On This Day.

I can hide nothing from you, Lord
So I won't even try
I need a re-commitment
Lord, you know the reason why.
Lord, Please Revive Me.

Jesus, help me to be bold
To stand up for what is right
As I walk and daily talk
May your word on me shed light.
Lord, Please Revive Me.

Faced with many decisions
And I know right from wrong
So, give me inner peace
As I join the Christian throng.
Lord, Please Revive Me.

Faith – Some Will Say

Some will say,
I thought I could do it
But I know I cannot.
There are too many obstacles
And for this I am fraught.

Some will say,
I'm so limited
It's too difficult for me to go.
There's no use in my trying
For I am too slow.

Some will say,
Well, I think I will quit
So, I won't ever have to worry.
For my troubles will be over
Because my stamina will be killed in a hurry.

Some will even say,
They tell me to have faith
Oh, I have a little bit.
But I need much more faith
And so, I'll just stop and quit.

BUT

Then, from deep within – faith appears
And gives me a surge and a try.
I was pleasantly surprised and truly blessed
And I kissed doubt good-bye.

Open The Door

Someone is knocking at your door
Can you hear it?
Hush, Hush, Hush
Someone is knocking – or will you fear it?

Open the door
There's a need to share.
And a need to care
Open the door.

Hear the man and woman begging
They are hungry and cold.
Hear them begging
They have a story to unfold.

Your fridge is running over
With lots of food inside.
Your shelves are all stocked
And there is nothing you can hide.

My closet is full of clothes
I cannot wear.
In my mind I keep saying
I'll wear them next year.

There are socks of all colors
That have been laid to rest.
Those with different odd designs
Stuffed in the cedar chest.

Now on the closet floor
Are all kinds of shoes.
Some of them matching
Ignoring the rules.

Why am I waiting?
To share these items with others.
I am prepared and now ready
To share with my sisters and brothers.

With so many surplus items
I keep holding on.
That's selfish and thoughtless
In fact it's so wrong.

With God's blessings upon me
I have too much stuff.
And there are many people near me
Who don't have enough.

Now it's inventory time
I'll give myself an exam.
I'm going to focus now
And really see where I am.

I am blessed, truly blessed
With so many worldly things.
Food, clothes and all kinds of items
That money usually brings.

So I ask myself right now
Why am I holding on?
To so very much that I don't need
Being selfish like this is so wrong.

So Lord, here I am today
Please search my selfish heart.
If there is wickedness in me
From it help me to depart.

I am sorry for being so selfish
I have much more than I need.
If I share my possessions with others
It will minimize some of my greed.

Lord, please forgive me
Of all of my selfish ways.
Help me now to share willingly
And give You the praise.

I do feel better now
For taking this step of generosity,
Selflessness and truth.
Of seeking forgiveness and trusting you Lord
As I become a caring and sharing Ruth.

I open the door.

Troubled Waters

Somewhere it's plainly said
God's gonna trouble the water.
With that being said, I have been led
To assess the waters, its impact,
And how we are to tread.

So we step calmly in the water
Which appears quiet and serene.
But looking at it frankly
The situation seems not so clean.

"God's Going To Trouble The Water"

With our life goals set before us
Though they're on the water's other side.
To reach our destination
We need a very strong guide.

Realistically our goals before us
Laid out on the other side.
To reach that destination
We've got to ride with the tide.

The troubled waters and tide can be a
Blessing even with muddy blunders.
They are all a part of God's marvelous plan
And the many wonders.

The waters of wonders and blunders
Are waiting to be stirred.
They are calm and unattractive
Just hesitating for the word.

The waters may be troubled
At times, they may not be still.
Some waters are patient and pensive
And just waiting for God's will.

Tranquil may seem like the water
And oh, so serene.
But when we glance again
Dirty pebbles can be seen.

Yes, the pond like life is a blessing
It's a mixture of the good and bad.
Sometimes we are supremely happy
And at other times we're gloomy and sad.

"Troubled Waters –
But God's Going To Trouble the Water"

Now as we gaze down at the water
Dirty rocks and stones we behold.
Many reveal corruption, hate and selfishness
Much we feel cannot be controlled.

Oh, the slow-moving tide is enticing
But the water is consumed with rocks.
And to get those rocks eliminated
We need to clear away the blocks.

The troubled water I'm observing
Yes, those dreaded pebbles are in the way.
In fact, the pebbles need a cleaning
From their despicable decay.

"So God's Going To Trouble The Water"

Now the water is quietly chanting
And there still is my goal.
Yet the water is being troubled
And waiting to unfold.

The waters can't stand still
They are troubled so they will move.
Arrogance, greed, a heartened heart
God does disapprove.

"So God's Going To Trouble The Water"

Life cannot stand still
The evidence of this is certainly great.
Involved we see the still and troubled water
Nonetheless, God's promises we await.

Our goals are still awaiting
And they are on the peaceful side.
We need to address the challenges
And let the troubled waters subside.

For God is troubling the waters
As we go through the stream.
There are circumstances in the way
That interrupt our plans
And a come-to-life dream.

For God is going to bless undoubtedly
And put all to the test.
As we travel the troubled waters.
For He truly knows what's best.

For the water pond of life is embedded
With its ups and downs.
And our blessings are pouring in
From so many rounds.

"Wherever Troubled Waters Do Flow"

When we look at the enticing tide
To get the rocks out of the way.
We must sift through the
Murky waters of rocks
And the dirt that they weigh.

*"We Need To Let
Troubled Waters Come Through"*

Aspirations do wait
Lying serenely on the other side.
The waters may be troubled
We must exercise patience as
The heavy waves subside.

Life is not always easy
It has its many twists and turns.
That water holds many uncertainties
And some unpredictable concerns.

*"To Get Our Attention –
God Troubles The Waters"*

In looking at life and in the mirror
Life, like the water, may seem appealing.
Upon closer observation
The rocks in the water are quite revealing.

There are many times in life
When things seem to be going well.
And then all at once we sense troubled waters
And experience some form of hell.

Sometimes we get so
Unappreciative and complacent
The waters need to be stirred.
We need now some troubled water
So God's voice can be heard.

There's a need for troubled water
For God speaks in different ways.
He desires that we seek Him
And give Him all the praise.

When God troubles the water
Action then takes place.
When God troubles the water
We should give God his space.

When God troubles the water
Let's gain insight and learn about life's race.
We should totally submit ourselves
To God's absolute amazing grace.

"God's Going To Trouble The Water"

Stop And Pray

When I find myself a wondering
And my thoughts appear a blundering.
And I find myself a plundering
What do I do next?
Stop and Pray.

When I can't find my keys anywhere
And I thought I had put them just right here.
But they don't seem to be anywhere near
What do I do next?
Stop and Pray.

When my thoughts appear to be rambling
And my focus is risky like gambling.
Rushing here – movement there – I'm scrambling
What do I do next?
Stop and Pray.

What happened to my personal empowerment?
And my ability and leadership endowment.
As I seek for myself and others – betterment
What do I do next?
Stop and Pray.

Where is my built up confidence?
When things just don't seem to make sense.
And the struggle sometimes seems so intense
What do I do next?
Stop and Pray.

Trust God and His faithfulness
Keep on learning and preparing for each test.
On the way coming is your success
As you Continue to PRAY.

Problems will remain on which you must cope
But your faith must develop as you find your hope.
God has your back, so hold on to the rope.
God is there saying, *"Continue to PRAY"*.

"My answer for you is coming", HE says
Yes, No, or Wait, our God portrays.
That's why we have to keep on
Giving HIM the praise.

KEEP ON PRAYING!!!

I Can't Breathe

I can't breathe
You blocked my air
You took my life away
Because you didn't care.

I can't breathe
My life and life-line are waning
I visualize my family – calling for them
For this treatment you imposed is distaining.

I can't breathe
It certainly isn't fair
Not giving me an opportunity
For a new outlook – some clean fresh air.

I can't breathe
There is no oxygen here
My rights have all been taken away
You want me to die in fear.

I can't breathe
You insist on keeping me down
Watching my breath being snuffed out
Killing me round by round.

I can't breathe
That's your way of saying to us
You have no kind of rights
So there's no need for you to fuss.

I can't breathe
Your feelings are quite evident
You heard me cry, you watched me die
Your racial message has been sent.

I can't breathe
This is a wake-up call
That we must seek justice
For one and for all.

For justice now
And for justice when
We behold and witness mistreatment
Of innocent women and men.

I can't breathe
Is a challenge to all
We should be involved and concerned
Of society's fall.

I can't breathe
My brother is dying
I can't breathe
Can't you hear him crying?

I can't breathe
For him I'm sighing
I can't breathe
We must continue trying and flying.

The South Carolina state motto says
"While I breathe, I hope"
We can say and pray
Let me breathe so I can cope.

Turn The Lights On

There are crumbs under the table and dirt under the rug
Spider webs around that can be easily found
And little eager children awaiting a hug.
Turn the lights on.

Some had unpleasant histories with terrible times as upward they grew
Like a bound slave who tried to be brave
But his freedom was an ugly clue.
Turn the lights on.

Horrific ways were hidden and treated that this generation did not know
How some people were mistreated and diabolically unseated
Their crushed feelings dared not show.
The lights need to be turned on.

Some circumstances in the dark and the gloomy touch was never told
Shadowed events with blackened indents
Crushed the courageous, brave, and bold.
The lights were not turned on.

With times and liberation moving forward and still seeing crumbs on the floor
The world needs to see the light
And do what's right through an open clear door.
So, turn on the lights.

Indeed, we are ashamed of ugly past events
Of how terrible we've been treated
Even when some doors were closed and facts exposed.
The lights needed to be on.

Is the "hush, hush" fair when you are keeping the truth out?
It's incredibly sad and politically bad
When many minds are full of doubt.
Turn the lights on.

Sometimes it's not so easy to swallow a big, elongated pill
But after several lapses and nauseous gasps
It will be there no longer still.
Finally, the lights were turned on.

That pill had to dissolve; it wasn't an easy thing to do
But through that dark, simply shown spark
The pill went reluctantly through.
The lights needed to be turned on.

We can't really hide our past; society needs to know
The truth, whole truth, hidden in the dark
The booth where the crumbs will later show.
When the lights are turned on.

Yes, segregation was politically wrong; we hate thinking of degradation
That terrible aggravation and unfair separation
Caused civil agitation within our divided nation.
Because the lights were not turned on.

Now some people think and try to prove that some cultures and their races
Are superior fanatics, using unjust tactics
Trying to keep in the dark without a spark, unexposed and dirty places.
Turn the lights on.

A little innocent child may say,
"Wow! I'm in here all alone I want to see how to be free
So please cut all the lights on."
Please turn the lights on.

Don't cut out this and leave out that OR try to hide something under a hat
Just tell the story like it is, though it may bring some salty tears
God's word is true, and I believe that.
Turn the lights on.

When you cut on the light, darkness will disappear
But truth wants to be heard and given the right word
But darkness likes to stay in the rear.
Let's turn the lights on.

Darkness cannot stay with the truth
The truth will eventually come to light
Whether sick or well, we just can't tell – but truth will surely win the fight.
So, keep the lights on.

Some people are selfish and quite inhumane – showing little respect
Their doors they want to close and fakingly publicly pose
And we really don't know what to expect.
Keep the lights on.

Openness is one thing, leading us to be free
For nothing surpasses true integrity
By opening the door and exposing the sore.
And letting the light in; that is key.

Turn the lights on and listen to the horn
Turn the lights on and see true freedom born
Tell all the truth, let it be known.
Tell all the whole truth, let the bright lights be shown.

Turn on the lights for we all need to know
From whence come our blessings
That will constantly grow.
The lights – turn the lights on.

True light gives one courage; true light gives one strength
That's why the light's dimensions
Have endless width and endless length.
Turn the lights on.

So, turn the lights on
This light power comes from above
It's a reflection of God's greatness and the strength of his love.
So, turn the lights on.

Keep On Keeping On

Sometimes it may be difficult
When you're doing your very best
To help someone along the way
To pass a struggling test.
Keep prodding away –
Just keep on keeping on.

You may sacrifice and struggle
And leave some personal things undone
Trying to help another
Release some burdens on their run.
Keep pushing them –
Just keep on keeping on.

But it hurts my very soul
When weariness steps in
And the "would-be" person who is struggling
Can't seem to make another bend.
Keep encouraging them –
Just keep on keeping on.

Urge them to take a break
But don't let them give up
Let them know that it is only
Just a crack in the cup.
We can get another cup –
Just keep on keeping on.

While life is hard and tempting
The end is not far away
Pause a bit and quietly sit
And begin your new found sway.
Renew your struggling efforts –
Just keep on keeping on.

Useful time is good and encouraging
It puts new life towards your goal
Remember your vying and keep on trying
And unlock the key marked "hold".
Keep on keeping on.

CHAPTER
3

Think On These Things
– Revelations

As revelations are depicted, disarmament is in order...
and awareness blossoms

Captivating The Fruits Of The Spirit

In order to grow strong
There are fruits we need to use.
They are Biblical statements given
From which we are to choose.

In the book of Galatians
Check out Chapter 5.
Verses 22 and 23
List fruit on which we can thrive.

These important lines
Give Fruits of the Spirit.
They are all plainly stated
And should be used and rightly fitted.

The first fruit listed is *"Love"*
And that is saying a lot.
For love affects us all
From an aged man down to a baby tot.

It's one of the first appealing fruits
And it comes from heaven above.
It should always be displayed
For there is nothing like true love.

"Joy" follows love
And for that we all should pray.
For this fruit tells us quietly
Of what we see and say.

From the tone of our voice
And that pleasant look.
Joy is a language portrayed
In our non-verbal facial book.

Along with our many other traits
That guide us along the way.
Is the fruit of *"Long-suffering"*
That faces us day by day.

Not giving up so soon
When an obstacle appears.
But take the issue whatever it is
And stay with it until it clears.

A fruit that is quite interesting
And has calmness you can feel.
Is the sweet loving touch
It is *"Gentleness"* that is real.

Focusing on gentleness
That's a special kind of touch.
Which is a welcome fruit
And it is needed so very much.

It may be hard to get to heaven
Without goodness on your side.
For *"Goodness"* is so enticing
And it'll take us for a God-given ride.

Goodness versus badness
Makes a person stand up tall.
Goodness is demonstrated
And responds to a Christly call.

What can be more satisfying
Than having *"Peace"* of mind.
Knowing that you have pleased God.
In doing His will so sublime.

When God speaks to us
Sometimes through meditation.
Peace comes and tells us what to do
When we follow God's dictation.

This answer will surely come
Having "*Faith*" that is sure.
For believing and trusting God
Our problems God surely can endure.

Because God promised us
His word we should believe.
Therefore, our faith should be so strong
His promises we will receive.

We are told to grasp "*Meekness*"
For if we are humble, we can win.
For the Bible instructs us to show
Meekness to all men.

Meekness is a virtue
And lowliness is the key.
We should follow Christ's example
Who demonstrated humility.

Being able to check one's self
And the temper it can hold.
Remaining calm and attentive
Now that is "*Self-control*".

When negative circumstances arise
And we are tempted to react.
The self-control spirit says
Be calm and use some tact.

Those Fruits of the Spirit
Are fruits we need to eat.
By eating them all when hunger does call
Our temperament will be near complete.

Physically speaking
Fruits improve our intake.
Spiritually speaking
If we don't eat now – that can be a mistake.

We grow from eating
And following The Word.
The Fruits of the Spirit
Should be obeyed when heard.

Of the nine listed fruits
Where do you stand?
Just check yourself eating
Then join the Spiritual Fruits clan.

What If?

I am just an inquiring teenager
Who is eager to explore.
What the world is about
Not too far from my door.

Yes, I am eager to see the world
Just like adults used to do.
They wanted to explore the surroundings
And get a bird's eye view.

Well, I have a group of friends
And we have social media too.
iPhones, Instagram, Facebook
And other media that grew.

There's nothing like your peers, I thought
And having some special friends.
Oh boy, did we have laughs and fun
And all kinds of grins.

We planned and plotted together
About things we would do.
Hoping we'd never get caught
Wondering if anyone would get a clue.

There was nothing so terrible going on
But we'd have fun and play jokes.
Clown around and act silly
And see reactions of the serious folks.

Just go back a few of your years
A few years down the road.
Just think of your numerous mistakes
And the "What If's" of life's load.
What If? What If?

I should not have done this – I should not have done that
I'm now reflecting on those interesting times.
My focus is now on moving forward
And seeking to learn as I climb.

What if I am traveling the wrong road?
I can now straighten up my act.
By getting off the "What If" mantra
And getting on the "I Will" track.

As I Think

If a man thinketh in his heart
So is he – if you believe.
You can receive
Then, you will achieve.

As a man thinketh – As I think

What did the little engine say
Though it was an upward way.
The hill is high and not close by
But I can make it if I try.

As a man thinketh – As I think

We all may have challenges
Dealing with unfairness and inequities.
But we must think positively
And commit to prayer in our heart and knees.

As a man thinketh – As I think

So as I think and think and think
While setting goals for ahead.
My planning can be a lesson for
Rebuking negativity and
Pessimistic thoughts unsaid.

As a man thinketh – As I think

Drugs

Unfortunately, drugs are taking over
And it's so sad to see
That they are leading evil in the world
And that hurts us desperately.

Drugs are killing people
The young and the old
There are many hidden stories
That are harmful and untold.

Getting high on drugs
Is a popular thing
And when the drugs go away
Then to what does one cling?

The good high feeling thing
Can't always be there
So use common sense
And let it be clear.

For God wants us to use
The smart brains in our head
And be productive people
And be intellectually fed.

Drugs may seem enticing
Yes, one may get high
But the high won't last always
Hopefully, the urge will fail and die.

We see and hear so many stories
We grieve at the mess we see
Sometimes we take actions
But many disregard our plea.

God challenges us to be faithful
And keep doing the best we can
Some will listen and try to follow
The lessons presented on demand.

Since drugs are so prevalent
And so very easy to get
We find our drug infested battle
Is a dangerous drug related threat.

Oh, it's so very discouraging
Sometimes it makes you want to cry
But your conscience says, "Keep on my child."
Let no one fool you, don't even try.

Our hearts go out when we behold
And see so very much
Sweet innocent children being drug exposed
And denied the human touch.

And then some children are directed
To leave their milk and honey
To go there, here, and yonder
And make some easy drug money.

These ugly drug situations
That are staring us in the face
Challenge us to use our resources
To help fight off this bad drug race.

But what's done in the dark
Will one day come to light
The day will come and go
And then will come the night.

There are drugs on the streets
There are drugs in the schools
And many ignore and disregard
The written and posted civil rules.

One of the great concerns
And this really bothers me
How we have left our foundation and roots
And the sense of community.

We just all have to remember
And do the best we can
Remembering that God is in control
And He has a righteous plan.

Be Ye Lifted

Sometimes I feel helpless
I don't know what to do.
I turn on the television
But some programs I'd like to sue.

So, I sit down in my chair or
Go back to my bed
And I'll start pitying myself.
Thinking and reliving about
Books that I have read.

Instead of focusing on the positives
Negation takes its part.
I begin examining myself
And thinking how I should start.

I should begin right now
Regardless of the weather.
Reminiscing of the successes
And of how they came together.

What makes things work out?
And what makes things fail?
A positive must and a negative not
Don't feed those who assail.

There's nothing like the saying
And the true philosophy.
"I think I can, I know I can."
Let me just try and see.

I'll put away the adverse saying
That likes to pluck my mind.
I will not and I never will see
That there's nothing good on this ground.

With goodness and success at the door
We need to give it a try.
First, we should check our mindset
So that right thoughts would comply.

With the higher things of life
That are waiting for a clue.
Patiently, they are available
So, let's take a positive view.

Some seek to discourage you
And focus on the "cannots".
But there's a story of a lady
Of whom I never forgot.

Well, someone told her it couldn't be done
But, oh how wrong that was.
Before the lady knew, she really did thrive
And realized that she was actually
One of the stars.

With her positive mind made up
And with her goals set before.
She began working without any shirking.
And her focus and exceptional skills,
We had to adore.

For her life seemed easier
And things fell into place.
She saw success with each demanding test
Even though challenges she did face.

With time, effort, and prayer
And a mind determined to win.
She worked hard and listened to God
And she was lifted and victorious in the end.

I Can See – I See You

I see what others see – I see what others don't see
I see you sacrificing time
I see you sharing and I see you caring
I see you talking and I see you listening.

For some don't have time or have mountains to climb
I see you being different and making room for another
My eyes are open and I can see
I see beauty in others that is for real.

I see patience in you – the real, true deal
I see kindness in you as you sacrifice
I see love in you while giving advice
I see understanding in you, for those who are hurt.

I see cleanliness in you with purpose
And a strength for beginning to cope
I see new life in you
With life's circumstance, in you I see hope.

Is see sorrows cease, replaced by peace
I see faithfulness in you, and someone being kind
I see long-suffering in you
And that's not always an easy find.

I Can See – I See You

If I Can

There are so very many jobs
To be done everywhere
Jobs here, there, and very near
Jobs to be done, oh it's so clear.

They are staring me in the face
And they're staring at you too
Sometimes we turn and see them
But we ignore them looking at you.

Why won't I answer the call?
What's keeping me away?
Maybe my attitude and my lack of gratitude
Compels me to go astray.

My consciousness is talking to me
It's telling me I should give a helping hand
To any needy woman or man
And I will be blessed and fully understand.

We would feel so much better
If we would stop and observe the truth
The work may not be simple or fun
Let's focus whether a senior or youth.

So with a ready and made up mind
And a will to do what's right
Now it's time to start – with my willing heart
And begin now while it is light.

When pursing the "If I Can" phrase
Let's really mean it for each hour
He supports and He provides
God has given us the power.

Time waits for no man
So, the time frame is now
If you can, and upon demand
Begin the "If I Can" right now.

Give Me A Book

Reading is my thing
I can learn so very much
Please, give me a book.

Listening is my thing
I like hearing good things
But, give me a book.

Walking is my thing
There is so much to see
But, give me a book.

Talking is surely my thing
There is so much to tell
But, give me a book.

Watching TV is my thing
For there is so much news
But, give me a book.

There are so many things to do
And so many places to look
I like doing all those things
But, I prefer reading a book.

Procrastination

Realizing it could have been
But I waited much too long
Procrastination took over
And washed away the strong.

Looking at the completed book
With all its printed pages
Doomed with pensive messages
Of various illustrative stages.

Lessons learned from books all there
Keep coming from my head
But lessons caught with endings naught
Went to sleep just like they were dead.

Visions and dreams slept all away
They were good on the smooth pillow
When daylight came with its glowing flame
They were usurped just like the willow.

Utilizing the present moment
Before it slips away
Daylight formed and the stars all roamed
And we wonder if they went astray.

Then looking at finished products
Many endings seem protected
But their different stages suffered
Through the ages
Though, partially accepted or
Carefully objected.

Upon reviewing our present status
We are recipients of numerous fights
Legally done and absolutely won
We kept fighting for our rights –
Halting procrastination .

Many roads were long and rugged
And there were hills and heights to climb
But determination and sure perseverance
Made these efforts all sublime.

Procrastination sought to interfere
And attempted to stop the progress
But the inner soul evaluates the toll
Which could have marred the total success.

Life truly has its ups and downs
And it's only human what we do
But it is a must for all of us
To keep working until we're through.

When are we through?
When do we rest?
When justice prevails
And our conscience entails.

Then we see answers to our quests
Some say, "I'll get it done tomorrow."
But tomorrow never comes
The work is still standing
Or has developed into crumbs.

So, procrastination has nothing to offer
It's a time killer in the way
It's a temporary excuse and mental abuse
And from it we should constantly stray.

Glancing at our success
And the work that has been done
Time secured, work endured
And many more races won.

Had we never started
There would be no finished work
Rather, pessimistic procrastination
And devious devastation.

So put procrastination behind you
It has no place for success
Its motto of, "Do It Later"
Indicates ruthless play and falsified jest.

Thanks for those trailblazers
Who saw and felt the need
Realizing the work to be done
Someone needs to take the lead.

So begin today this I pray
Affirm this needed elevation
Without hesitation or any reservation
Simply, bury procrastination.

Lateness

Why should I be late?
If I've long known the date
Who wants an unpleasant fate?
Or an undesirable time rate.

Is there really an excuse?
For lateness – no punctuality
This late habit can be licked
This late habit should be kicked.

For most everyone seeks the good
As all really should
Begin now this very day
Of being punctual in every way.

Who Am I? – I Am Ms. B.

I am Black, I am Beautiful, and I am Bold
Some of this you can see.
But I am grateful to be a part
of this Black History.

Who Am I? – I Am Ms. B.

I am brainy, I am brave, and I am bright
With this you may agree.
And it makes me mighty proud
To be a part of our Black History.

Who Am I? – I Am Ms. B.

I am a beaming bundle of joy
A branch from a Biblical tree.
My birthright and my blood
Proves my Black History.

Who Am I? – I Am Ms. B.

I'm a bonder with my brothers
Bonding helps our unity.
Bringing us closer together
To share our history.

I am benevolence to my sister
And buoyancy for my brother.
I am a builder of community and civil rights
And for that, I wouldn't trade for another.

Who Am I? – I Am Ms. B.

I am Blackness who survived the bulging storm
The fire and the brutal flood.
The one who is grateful for it all
And submissive to Jesus' precious blood.

Who Am I? – I Am Ms. B.

I am breath to the breathless
Though some may try to keep me down.
But God has my Back and Blackness
And for that I am heaven bound.

Who Am I? – I Am Ms. B.

Seeing Your Good And God

There is something good in you
And I see it sparkling through.

There's a pleasant smile on your face
It lights up brightly just in the right place.

I sense how hard you're trying
And how very high you are flying.

I just love the way you're greeting
All the people you are just meeting.

There's something in your tone of voice
That seems to make a heart rejoice.

Your radiance of service shines through
I see your good and God in you.

Sharing And Caring

Lord, please search my heart today
For I know that you hear.
I don't have to talk so loud
I'm a witness that you care.

Though some may talk with volume
And have much strength in their voice.
My prayer for myself and others
Is that we make a Godly choice.

I am a rather quiet person
And perhaps not extremely
Swift on the tongue.
But I want to share what's on my heart
For the poor and needy one.

When it comes to making provisions
And there is much to be done.
I'm concerned that we don't
Care enough for others
Of our blessings that have come.

God Wants Us To See

It' a sad, sad day when our eyes are shut
And we can't even see
We can pray, listen and hear
But we can't see.

There may be flowers of many different colors
Flowers and leaves of different shapes
You may hear one talking about their beauty
But you can't see them.

You may listen well and visualize their beauty
In odd-shaped vases which may be placed
In various places
Where their visibility can't be missed
But you still can't see them.

Just as the beauty in those flowers are there
And you can't see them
There are blessings and beauty in your life
And we can see them.

We can feel them; we can appreciate them
Though you say not a word
They are not hidden
But we can see them and they are heard.

Oh, how grateful for our eyes
To behold beauty to see what others see
Forbearance and gentleness
Are very clear to me
When I see them expressed so explicitly.

God gave me my eyes
And I am blessed to see
So may blessings in others
With such positivity.

God gave us all eyes
And He wants us to see
The good in others
Expressed humanely.

CHAPTER
4

A Spoonful
Of Humor

It is said that laughter is good for the soul; a merry heart is good medicine (Proverbs 17:22). I agree, for laughter adds joy. Try it at some moment in your life (perhaps today) as you allow laughter to sooth your soul.

Chores And The "Need-To-Relax" Touch

My parents had eight children
Five boys and the girls made three.
We got along rather well together
But, occasionally, we'd disagree.

Like, who'd get the most peanuts?
Or who deserved the longest candy cane?
Or who shelled the most peas?
And who was the most insane?

Who should wash the dishes?
And who should sweep the floor?
Who should put the clothes up?
And do other little chores galore.

The older boys did the rough work
The girls supposedly worked inside.
But I, they say, did much of nothing
And I'd go somewhere and hide.

I did a pretty good job of that
Of getting out of their way.
I'd stay away from doing chores
And go somewhere and play.

And so until this very day
I will only do but so much.
When chores try to dictate to me
I use my "Need-To-Relax" touch.

Couz's Funeral

I'm Aunt Ruth – all dressed and ready to go
In my navy blue outfit and big white hat.
In case someone questioned why I wore that
I could push them aside and tell them to scat.

My car tank was already filled with gas
Of course, I knew where the funeral was.
Tissue, purse, and Bible in the car
I had to get there for my Couz.

I had no time to sit around and talk
For I surely didn't want to be late.
A good seat up front was my desire
As I was not one who liked to wait.

Today, I won't be a late number
For I'm determined to be on time.
That's why I got ready so early
Cause I wanted my seat to be prime.

So I hurriedly walked past a lady
Who was walking oh, so slow.
I asked her to please excuse me
Perhaps she was in the wrong church row.

And then this same lady paced before me
I noticed how jittery she was.
She said she was in the family
And the deceased was her Couz.

"Me, too", I responded quickly
"Well, what was your cousin's name?"
"Oh, we just call her 'Couz' for short"
"That was her name game."

You tell me where Couz lived, I asked
And what was her favorite food?
No answers from the lady
So I'm getting suspicious, but I don't want to be crude.

More questions I began to ask her
As the lady is fumbling for sure.
My line of inquisitiveness and questioning
She clearly did not want to endure.

Lady, you are strange and curious
And something is not quite right.
Just listening to you up close and near
Something is a little shady –
I need some insight.

First, you don't know who's dead
You don't even know the decease's name.
You don't know where the deceased lived
I'm wondering now are you a scam and a game.

In fact, something is extremely interesting
You kept talking about Couz – "her" lifespan.
You didn't even know that lying before us
Is the body of a "man".

Daddy's Solution

The tag game was oh so interesting
And so were those active boys.
But those friends of his sons kept their game
And they were enjoying their noise.

They weren't worried about behavior
Nor about toning their voices down.
Their noise was their noise –
The noise of the boys
For they were determined to have fun
And clown around.

Little attention did the grown folks pay me
About what my father said.
My friends insisted on doing their thing
And louder their hollers were led.

My father gave me a final warning
"Stop your noise or your answer I'll find.
Tell me, son, what will happen to you
If I take off this belt of mine?"

"Oh, that's very easy, Daddy."
His son's voice was calm and soft.
"If you take that belt off from around your waist
Your pants would surely fall off."

Dr. Seuss

Dr. Seuss – Dr. Seuss
Your illustrations are true.
What makes you
Do like you do?

You write in a rhyme
Most of the time.
I'm not complaining
I think that's fine.

It helps me with my phonics
When I try to sound.
But I get tickled
And laugh like a clown.

Your books are funny
They are free and loose.
Nobody writes like you
Dr. Seuss – Dr. Seuss.

I like your books
Like a bear likes honey.
Dr. Seuss – Dr. Seuss
You are alluring and funny.

Your writing is captivating
And has stood the test of time.
To know you is to really like you
For you are truly long-standing prime

Chicken Feet

I like different kinds of foods
And all kinds of meat.
But I surely don't like and won't even try
To eat any cooked chicken feet.

My Mother has tried to make me
Eat those four-toed things.
I don't care how she seasons them
They are far from chicken wings.

She puts many different seasonings in them
To spruce up the taste.
But I let her know and actually show
To me, that's actually a waste.

Just the idea of chicken feet
With those four toes on the yard.
Doesn't set well with me at all
And I am on my guard.

She may try something else
Some other foods, I may greet.
But please help my Mother to know
That I detest CHICKEN FEET.

Peanut Butter And Some Jelly

I was enjoying a beautiful, sunny day
Filled with calm and serenity.
I was captivated in reading a book
For that surely is my cup of tea.

As hours went by, I took out my lunch
Of peanut butter and bread.
And my big bottle of Kool-Aid
All colored bright and red.

After eating a little of the sandwich
I decided to take a short nap.
And when I woke up standing beside me
Was a big blob of jelly in a wrap.

I asked the jelly what's the problem
He said, "Well I feel left out".
I looked at him with a quizzical face
As he had a jelly pout.

I replied that I can
Surely take care of that – no fight.
I grabbed a slice of bread
And the jelly I gobbled in delight.

For I am not one to allow you
To feel unwanted and overlooked.
Due to unity, inclusion, and togetherness
That peanut butter AND JELLY had me hooked.

Super Bowl Sunday

Super Sunday!
Super Bowl!
Super gathering
Good for the soul.

Loving family and loving friends
They look forward to getting together
Enjoying football
Regardless of the weather.

What do you superly do?
At this special super time?
Oh, we laugh, we talk, and we watch the game
And while doing this, we also dine.

What do we eat? We rarely guess
Because it really does not matter
Whatever is available
It comes along with our super chatter.

You are free to root for your team
The one you really care about
How they got to the Super Bowl
Fate must have won their super clout.

Now some of us like to watch the game
And some like to super talk
But do what makes you happy here
So do your thing in your Super Bowl walk.

Now whether you call it Bowl Day
Or prefer calling it Super Bowl Sunday
We're pleased to have your presence
For this is better than any Saturday matinee.

Football draws people together
And we like to coach from our chair
We criticize and call the plays
And we judge the game penalties that aren't fair.

But it's all good we do agree
This super Super Bowl
Just talking, laughing and listening
Hearing the truth and stretched stories being told.

So, for Super Bowl Sunday – blessings on Team A
And hoorah for Team B
Thanks for bringing us together
For we welcome the food, laughter, and fun rivalry.

Wow!
What A Girls' Basketball Game!

Oh, how tired and worn I was
For I had only slept 3 hours from the night before.
I was truly in need of rest
And had a really loud snore.

My list of things to do
Was getting longer each and every day.
Committed to tasks for sure
I had a plan for work and play.

Despite what I had to do
I just had to watch my girls' game.
Oh, they have such a fantastic record
Ready and talented is their claim.

So hurriedly I completed one task
And began with another.
I was determined to prepare for the girls' game
So I got my pillow and favorite cover.

I glanced at the clock for a minute
And I had just 30 minutes before the game race.
I could get a few more things done
As my "To Do" list kept staring me in the face.

My cell phone insisted on ringing
But I just let it ring on off the hook.
I refused to try to answer it
For I just knew it was another spam crook.

Now, I just had 10 more minutes
That I could rest until then.
Without a single fussy disturbance
But a peaceful moment was mine herein.

And then that old disrespectful phone
Suddenly woke me up.
And my sleepy, quenched eyes popped open
Knocking over the tea in my cup.

Wow! It's almost game time, I thought
The hands on the clock showed the circling border.
The scoreboard on the TV announced
"Only 5 seconds left in this fourth quarter."

Something Happened On The Lawn

Two active groups of boys
Each appeared on a different side.
Of a big and long-playing lawn
That was open, green, and wide.

Then one group started running
And the other group did too.
Then they all fell down
And I couldn't tell who was who.

Afterwards, they seemed to be praying
In a huddle, but not in a line.
They put their heads together
I was hoping that they were all safe and fine.

Then, they got up and started running
Both groups fell down on the ground.
And there was much noise from a lot of people
And shouts from all around.

Then the groups sat down for a little while
They then stood slowly to their feet.
Perhaps they were trying to decide
If they should reverse and take a seat.

So, I watched, looked, and listened
Trying to find out what was going on.
I wondered and I pondered
About this grouping on this lawn.

No one explained to me
About this mystery.
Was this an unusual phenomena?
That was somehow meant to be.

I was really curious and upset
About this lawn group situation.
I'm still looking for the FBI
For a timely explanation.

Lady, Don't Follow Me

Down Main Street I was walking
And I glanced over to my left.
I saw a strange bent over lady
Who looked slightly unkept.

She had on an old-fashioned, ragged hat
That really didn't look so clean.
In fact, I wouldn't have worn it
For I would not want to be seen.

I kept creeping along and thinking
And then I discovered something new.
There were beautiful items along the outside shop
And as I stopped, the lady stopped too.

I wondered why she stopped when I stopped
For I don't want to talk to her.
She's really not my kind of person
Movement in another area I really would prefer.

So I reached into my pocket
And she did the very same.
Then I shook my fist at her
And I thought, "What an interesting dame."

I continued to walk a little farther
Casting my eyes in her direction.
The lady looked at me and I returned the look
I'm wondering now if I need protection.

To myself, I thought alone praying
The lady needs to go and sit down.
For if she isn't very cautious
She's going to soon hit the ground.

I balled up my fist at her and frowned
Then I threw her a right arm punch.
She did the very same to me
And the pavement was our crippled crunch.

"Oops, Wow, Oops", we mutually grunted
And we looked each other in the eye.
As we fell, we were both able to tell
That mirrors never lie.

Watch Out, Driver

Watch out, driver, please
Don't you see me?
I'm driving in the middle of the road
Because I want to be free.

I don't want to be hit
On my left side or my right.
I don't want to be hit
I'm not in for a fight.

That's why I try to stay
Right in the middle of the road.
But if you happen to hit me
You'll have to pay a heavy load.

Don't you see me coming?
You'd better get out of my way.
Or I'll call the police
And have you sent away.

You see, driving in the middle of the road
Is actually good for me.
I can see on my right and my left quite clearly
And talk and wave to all in the community.

I really don't understand the problem
For I think I'll present a law and petition.
Let's all drive in the middle of the road
It's a wonderful driving position.

ACKNOWLEDGEMENTS

There are many individuals of whom I feel so very indebted for the successful publication of this book – *"Poetic Outpouring Thoughts"*. It is impossible to list them all. I will, however, mention a few persons who have been extremely instrumental as I pursued this publication effort. These individuals (along with others) were most helpful – inclusive of their prayers and encouragement.

I acknowledge my three lovely, helpful and talented daughters, along with their spouses – Dr. Marshalita Sims Peterson and Dr. Alan Peterson, Evangelist Kemolet Sims Mitchell and Rufus Mitchell, and Terutha Rachelle Sims. Terutha and Kemolet provided exemplary logistical support involving the publication project. I also acknowledge the following individuals.

- Stephanie Fontenot, my Goddaughter, who provided technical support with much patience;

- Mrs. Beatrice McDonald who readily and helpfully supplied her stenographic skills;

- Bishop David Tompkins, Sr. for the provision of photographic setting/location;

- The Columbia Writers Alliance of which I am a member and wherein is directed by Mrs. Jerlean Noble, who constantly encouraged and checked on my progress;

- Dr. Cathine Scott, a writing advocate, who wholeheartedly supported me and also facilitated national publication of one of my poems;

▦ Dr. Josie Bright-Stone who provided all-around support during the book project;

▦ Mrs. Ida Williams Thompson, my friend and mentor who was once my student during her high school years but emerged as my district wide Library Director and a constant source of inspiration and support.

Lastly, Deborah Ruth Mitchell, my granddaughter (quite a talented young lady), provided exceptional technical support along with facilitation of photographic activities. I acknowledge Darwin McJimpsey (my grandson-in-love) along with his gifted and supportive wife, Dr. Alana Peterson McJimpsey (my granddaughter). Darwin and Alana provided superb services involving their innovation, creativity and quality throughout the publication process. As a professional Graphic Arts Designer, Darwin utilized his expert technical skills to support me. He and Alana designed and supplied all graphics for this project along with co-facilitation of the publishing process (alongside Marshalita). Marshalita was my major assistant who astronomically and constantly encouraged, critiqued, edited, organized, researched and guided the entire publication process. She engaged in outstanding facilitation of this project – such that POTS came to fruition.

"THANK YOU" – YOU ARE TRULY APPRECIATED !!!

ABOUT THE AUTHOR

Esther Ruth Butler Sims is a prominent poet, educator, community / civic volunteer, ministry worker, and historian. She is an inspirational, high impact visionary and transformational leader. She has a distinctive career that has been marked by a host of positions at several educational and community levels. She held teaching positions at the elementary, middle, and high school levels in South Carolina (Richland County School District One and beyond). Mrs. Sims has over 55 years of service in public education. She also served as librarian at Benedict College and the Richland County Public Library (all in Columbia, SC / metro Columbia, SC).

Mrs. Sims has had intensive intellectual preparation and study. She holds a Master's Degree of Library Science from North Carolina Central University (Durham, NC) and a Bachelor of Arts Degree in English from Benedict College (Columbia, SC). She has engaged in further studies through the University of South Carolina (Columbia, SC), Simmons College (Boston MA), and Columbia College (Columbia, SC).

The are many "firsts" associated with Esther Ruth Butler Sims. She has been a trailblazer and pioneer in the Richland County School District (Columbia, SC) as the first female of color to hold leadership positions. She was the first chairperson of Richland School District One Librarians Department. She is one of three (3) Blacks in Richland School District One to integrate schools. Esther Ruth Butler Sims was the first Black librarian to serve in a White school. She was a charter member of the Columbia Urban League Guild, serving as the first President.

Her commitment to serving Christ and mankind is remarkable. She is an active member of her church and has served in numerous church-related and ministry leadership roles. She is viewed by her peers as "A Woman of Great Faith" and a "Directress Emerita" because of the many positions she has held.

She has a scholarship named in her honor that provides financial support to youth throughout the state of South Carolina. A Bethel Christian Camp Scholarship has been named in honor of Esther Ruth Butler Sims for her camp service of over 35 years. She served as the only female on the Board of Bethel Bible Camp for over 15 years.

Esther Ruth Butler Sims is a member of several prestigious organizations inclusive of the National Council of Negro Women, National Council of University Women, Church Women United, and Columbia Urban League. She is also a golden member of Alpha Kappa Alpha Sorority, Inc. She has received numerous awards and certificates of appreciation such as the South Carolina Human Relations Award (Local, County, State Winner). She has been recognized nationally by community and church-related organizations due to her engaging membership, faithful work, dedicated service, and extra ordinary contributions to society.

Mrs. Sims is highly motivated, views challenges from a visionary perspective, and seeks creative solutions. She has motivated and impacted educators and young people around the world through her travels nationally and internationally (throughout Europe) and through her community, civic, and cultural engagements involving creative writing, storytelling, and poetry. Esther Ruth Butler Sims has authored over 100 poems. She penned "A Change is Coming" in January 2021 at the age of 90. This poem has received world-wide recognition by numerous organizations. It is published in the 2021 edition of the Journal of the Association of University Women.

At the age of 93, Esther Ruth Butler Sims is still very active, strong minded, comical, and a role model for young girls and women in her queenly-like manner, dress for success, and positive attitude toward life. She is blessed with a loving family, an embracing village, and outstanding supporters – all who continue to inspire her to be creative, determined, innovative, engaged, and visionary.

Made in the USA
Middletown, DE
02 October 2023

39983606R00046